FORT
WITH TAR

In the same series:

FORTUNE-TELLING BY PLAYING CARDS
Nerys Dee

FORTUNE-TELLING BY DICE
David and Julia Line

FORTUNE-TELLING WITH TAROT CARDS

STUART R. KAPLAN

AN ILLUSTRATED GUIDE TO SPREADING AND INTERPRETING THE 1JJ TAROT

PARRAGON

This edition published 1997 by Diamond Books for

Parragon
Units 13–17, Avonbridge Industrial Estate
Atlantic Road, Avonmouth
Bristol BS11 9QD

First published in the UK by the Aquarian Press as
Tarot Cards for Fun and Fortune Telling, 1978

First published by US Games Systems Inc. New York, 1970

Dedicated to my wife, *Marilyn*, and to our children
Mark, Peter, Michael, Christopher and *Jennifer*

ISBN 0 752 51950 6

Printed in Great Britain by
Caledonian International Book Manufacturing Ltd, Glasgow

CONTENTS

The illustrations and card designs used in this book are reprints from the original Tarot IJJ deck produced in Switzerland by Muller & Cie. Grateful appreciation is acknowledged to Muller & Cie for permission to reproduce these Tarot cards. The IJJ deck is distributed in this country by Waddingtons Playing Card Co Ltd and is available through normal retail outlets or direct from the publishers of this book.

PREFACE

This book has been prepared for use with the popular Tarot 1JJ deck produced for several centuries by Muller & Cie, Switzerland.

What are tarot cards? What is the origin and meaning of the word *tarot?* Can anyone really foretell the future with tarot cards? These are among some of the questions most frequently asked about the ancient pack of cards.

Tarot cards are believed to have originated in Italy about five centuries ago for several purposes: to provide a pictorial presentation of the times, to play a card game involving suit trumps, and to read and foretell the future. Several original tarot decks dating from the fourteenth century are today in the possession of museums and libraries as well as private collections. The word *tarot* appears to have originated during the fourteenth century in Italy in the word form of *tarocco* or *tarocchi*. Other words describing the cards include *tarok, taroc* and *tarock*.

The current resurgence of interest in occult and mystic phenomena, fortune telling, tarot cards, the supernatural, witchcraft and a wide spectrum of spiritualism has created an unprecedented interest in the Tarot 1JJ deck. *Fortune-Telling With Tarot Cards* is an invaluable aid to the follower of tarot who wishes to learn more about the deck itself, the meaning of the cards and the card spreads most frequently employed.

Can anyone really reveal fortunes with tarot cards? All of us possess conscious and subconscious reactions to symbolic pictures. The daughter of an Italian count in the fourteenth century amused her noble family with hand-painted pictorial tarot cards; in the sixteenth century a learned scholar in Germany delved into the hidden meaning of the tarot cards; Gypsies wandering throughout Europe for centuries offered the wisdom of the tarot to eager questioners; in the seventeenth century an aged hermit peered into the mysteries of the tarot through flickering candle light; in the courts of France a wigged King and his coterie carefully heeded the words of the cards; many cartomancers and diviners such as Mlle. Lenormand of France foretold great and catastrophic events to Napoleon; and in the nineteenth century learned men expounded upon the symbolic meanings of the mystic cards.

Today in many libraries and dens with electric lights and surrounded by modern technological advances, the mystery of the centuries-old tarot pack continues to be pursued. Some readings may be so accurate as to defy the rationale of the objective mind. Other readings may be so inaccurate and unresponsive as to offer little insight to the questioner. Are these the result of some mystic, symbolic wisdom or are they the extension of pure fantasy? Undeniably, the tarot deck enjoys a continuous history for more than 500 years and is the forerunner of today's modern pack of playing cards.

It is not the author's intention to expound any theory or to propose any viewpoint with respect to the possible authenticity of fortune telling with tarot cards. Instead, to those readers who find the Tarot 1JJ cards interesting, mystical, symbolical and challenging, let the cards speak for themselves.

New York
March, 1970

S. R. Kaplan

CHAPTER I — INTRODUCTION TO TAROT

Tarot cards are surrounded by a considerable amount of mystery and legend and the precise origin of the ancient cards is not known with certainty. Most followers of tarot believe that the cards originated in Europe in the fourteenth century. Others believe that the earliest use of tarot was in India, China or ancient Egypt in the form of clay tablets.

Several tarot decks are available today, all containing seventy-eight cards and, generally, each deck has the same or similar symbolic pictures. The interpretation of each pictorial tarot card is basically universal, limited only by the intuition and judgment of the Diviner or Reader. One of the most popular tarot decks, enjoying widespread acceptance in the United States during the current revival in occult and spiritual matters, is the ancient tarot deck 1JJ produced by Muller & Cie in Switzerland

During the fourteenth century in Italy a tarot pack was used to play a game called *tarocco*. The word *tarot* is the French adaptation of the word *tarocco*. The ancient 78-card tarot decks generally comprised fifty-six regular playing cards known as the Lesser Arcana, divided into four suits numbered 10 to 1 (or Ace) with a King, Queen, Cavalier and Page. Suit signs were the forerunners of today's suits:

Swords or Epees	=	Spades
Batons, Scepters or Wands	=	Clubs
Cups or Coupes	=	Hearts
Coins, Deniers or Pentacles	=	Diamonds

In addition to the fifty-six cards, the tarot decks contained twenty-two pictorial cards known as Trump, Triumph, Atouts, Greater Arcana, or the Major Arcana cards, numbered from XXI to I plus an unnumbered card known as "The Fool." Most people today are unaware that the ordinary pack of playing cards is a direct descendant from the fourteenth century tarot deck. As card playing increased in popularity the trump cards were dropped, the Cavalier and Page cards were combined into today's Jack, and "The Fool" became the Joker, thus giving us the standard deck of fifty-two cards plus joker.

The original game of tarot apparently was for three players and involved bidding, melding of points, and the taking of tricks. Although tarot games have varied considerably through the centuries, they have followed a basic pattern and are still played in some parts of Europe. The highest card of the suit takes the trick, unless it is trumped. Trumps rank from XXI high to I low. The dress cards (King, Queen, Cavalier, Page) rank from King high to Page low. The masculine suits of Swords (Spades) and Batons (Clubs) rank from 10 high to 1 (or Ace) low. However, the feminine suits of Cups (Hearts) and Coins (Diamonds) rank in reverse order: Ace (or I) high to 10 low. Points are added or subtracted depending upon the cards taken in each trick.

Several original and very old tarot decks are in the possession of museums and libraries. The Pierpont Morgan Library in New York City has thirty-five cards from a seventy-eight card tarot deck dating back to (circa) 1484 and believed to be the work of either Bonifacio Bembo or Antonio Cicognara, except for three cards painted by another artist.

The deck apparently belonged to Cardinal Ascanio Maria Sforza (1445-1505) or to his mother, Bianca Visconti Sforza. Eventually the deck became the property of the Colleoni family and Count Alessandro Colleoni exchanged twenty-six of the cards with his friend, Count Baglioni, in return for a portrait of one of Count Colleoni's ancestors. Upon the death of Count Baglioni the twenty-six cards were willed to the Accademia Carrara in Bergamo, Italy. The remaining cards, except for several that are missing, are today in the possession of the Colleoni family. The Sforza deck is painted on heavy cardboard and corresponds almost card for card to the modern tarot pack.

The Sforza cards were probably not intended for actual play and, instead, may have been merely visual representations of the times. Forty of the Lesser Arcana cards of the Sforza deck depict the symbols of Swords, Staves (scepters), Cups and Coins in the same number as is necessary to illustrate the number of the card, i.e. five cups depict the 5 of Cups.

This is the same system used in the Tarot 1JJ deck with the additional feature that each card in the Swiss deck is numbered in Roman numerals for easy identification.

In the archives at the Bibliotheque Nationale in Paris there are 17 Major Arcana cards believed to have been hand painted by Jacquenin Gringonneur for Charles VI of France in the late fourteenth century. Four other cards which may belong to this same set survive at the Museo Correr in Venice.

By the end of the fifteenth century the Italian tarot deck had undergone some modifications and throughout many cities of Europe the *Tarot of Marseille* deck—somewhat different in design but with the identical subjects—became widely popular. In local areas different decks were produced containing either 62 cards, 78 cards or 97 cards. The *minchiate* pack originating from an area near Florence contained a wealth of artistic detail in its 97 cards. The *minchiate* deck comprised 56 cards in four suits plus 41 trump cards consisting of the regular 22 Major Arcana cards plus 19 additional zodiac and astrological cards.

Through the centuries the 78-card tarot deck in its various forms has been used for fortune telling. In 1781 the French archeologist, Antoine Court de Gebelin, in his work *Jeu des Tarots* advanced the theory that tarot cards originated in Egypt and subsequently cards were printed with Egyptian pictures. However, these pictures generally follow the designs from decks used by wandering Gypsies in Europe.

During the period 1783 to 1787 Monsieur Alliette, a French wig maker, sought to modify and popularize the cards by producing several works and his own set of cards known as "Tarots d'Etteilla," a reversal of his name.

Numerous fortune telling cards were produced thereafter and in the early nineteenth century, Mlle. Lenormand came into high favor at the French court as a diviner. A beautiful reproduction of the exact Lenormand cards found after her death are produced by Muller & Cie in the original French and a similar version in English.

In the second half of the nineteenth century, Alphone Louis Constant, also known as Eliphas Levi, published several works on tarot including *Dogme et Rituel de la Haute Magie, Histoire de la Magie, La Clef des Grands Mysteres, Le Livre des Splendeurs, Clefs Magiques et Clavicules de Solomon* and *Le Grand Arcane*. Levi also designed a modified scientific pack of tarot cards.

In 1889 a learned Frenchman and physician, Gerard Encausse, known as Papus, set down in systematic fashion the keys to the tarot in his book, *The Tarot of the Bohemians.*

In 1910 Arthur Edward Waite wrote his well-known book, *The Pictorial Key to the Tarot* and he further redesigned the tarot cards into the Waite deck.

The Tarot 1JJ deck is believed to follow closely the original ancient packs and its authenticity makes it a valuable card pack for the collector or interested tarot follower.

The manner of spreading tarot cards for reading and the interpretations of the symbolic pictures on each card have changed through the centuries. Indeed, the precise art of spreading and reading the cards as may have been practiced centuries ago is lost. Nevertheless, there are several methods in use today which serve the purpose of the interested follower of tarot. It is possible that some day the precise art of spreading and reading tarot cards may again come to light through the chance investigations of an interested individual.

Each of the Major Arcana cards in the Tarot 1JJ deck carries a descriptive title and a symbolic picture. A combination of the title and picture of each card is intended to bring to the mind of the interpreter a series of events and/or ideas for his or her interpretation. The descriptive meanings assigned in this book to each of the Major Arcana cards, as well as the Lesser Arcana cards, should be used as a guide. Generally, the Major Arcana cards represent the physical and spiritual forces affecting man such as strength, power, storms, death and religion. The Lesser Arcana cards represent occupations, social position and status such as the aristocracy, upper class and executives represented by epees, swords and spades; the merchant and business class represented by deniers, coins and diamonds; the clergy and religious groups represented by the sacramental coupes, cups and hearts; and the peasantry and lower income class represented by batons and clubs. The Diviner should seek through practice to assign his own meanings to each of the cards.

Tarot cards cannot be read from two directions as conventional cards. If the card is upside down or inverted, then the meaning of the card is weakened, delayed or even reversed. The presence of one card next to another card strengthens or lessens the meaning of the cards combined. Readings are determined not only by taking into account the divinatory meaning of a specific card but also by relating the proximity in which cards fall in relation to each other, frequency of occurrence, frequency of the proximity between two or more cards, and whether the card is upside down.

The procedure described in this book for the spreading of the Tarot 1JJ pack requires that the Questioner (the person seeking an answer to a question) shuffle the cards face down while stating out loud his specific question to the Diviner or Reader. The Diviner then lays out the cards in the prescribed sequence and interprets the symbolic meanings of the cards. The individual should seek through practice to spread the cards in a manner which feels most comfortable.

Importantly, the readings of the cards may represent only a small portion of what the Questioner seeks to have answered. In fact, the question itself may serve merely as the starting point for a broad interpretation by the Diviner of the Questioner's present and future possibilities.

We are exposed to a vast amount of information in our daily lives and our conscious mind retains only a small portion. Our subconscious mind holds a wealth of extrasensory information, facts and impulses including the ability to associate ideas with symbols. Tarot cards offer the opportunity to utilize our conscious and subconscious abilities in the spreading and interpretation of the symbolic tarot cards in order to provide a way of looking at life in its present time and the possible extensions and directions which exist in the future.

It is suggested that persons using the Tarot 1JJ cards for fortune telling may find the twenty-two Major Arcana cards quite adequate without the need of the Lesser Arcana cards. However, should the individual also wish to utilize the Lesser Arcana cards, the Tarot 1JJ deck comprises the full seventy-eight cards.

CHAPTER II — THE MAJOR ARCANA CARDS

The Tarot 1JJ deck contains 78 cards in full color comprising what may be regarded as two separate decks: the twenty-two Greater Arcana cards and the fifty-six Lesser Arcana cards.

The twenty-two Major Arcana cards in numerical sequence with French titles, English titles, symbolic picture descriptions, suggested divinatory meanings and reverse meanings are as follows:

(Unnumbered Card)
LE MAT — THE FOOL

DESCRIPTION: A gaily attired young man pauses momentarily at the edge of a precipice. The abyss at his feet holds no terror for him. His face expresses disarming innocence. He is a jester dressed in gorgeous red, yellow and blue vestments and he wears a conical foolscap with ornamental pompons. In his right hand he holds a wand, symbol of his spirit and enthusiasm. His cap, shirt, pants, leggings and shoes are divided into two colors—red and blue—signifying extravagance. His collar, shirt and knee garters are scalloped and his cap and garters have pompons which when in motion suggest frenzy. The fool is a prince in another world of fun and fascination. He is about to enter the supreme adventure. He represents inexperience and naivete seeking self-expression. He is the creative person about to savor the freshness of the morning of life.

DIVINATORY MEANING: This card signifies folly. Immaturity. Foolishness. Irrationality. Frivolity. Levity. Thoughtlessness. Lack of consideration. Rashness. Lack of discipline. Extravagance. Ridiculous expenditure or act. Delirium. Craze. Infatuation. Passion. Obsession. Mania. Indiscretion. Unrestrained excess. The person drawing this card must be careful to use his will power to overcome foolishness and to make the right choice in life.

REVERSE MEANING: The reverse meaning of this card is to make a faulty choice. Choose the wrong road. Halt or hesitate in life's progress. Apathy. Negligence.

LE MAT — THE FOOL
(Unnumbered Card)

I LE BATELEUR —
THE MAGICIAN OR THE JUGGLER

DESCRIPTION: A magician or juggler in a wide-brimmed hat stands before various objects placed at random upon a table. Through his cleverness and creativity the magician must rearrange the objects. The magician's upraised left hand holds a magic wand toward the heavens and his right hand points downward towards earth. This dual sign suggests that all things are derived from above to create all things on earth. The unity of will seeks to combine into creativity. The magician's innocent smile suggests that through his inner knowledge he has the power to bring things into manifestation.

DIVINATORY MEANING: This card symbolizes originality. Spontaneity. Imagination. Self-reliance. Resolution. Skill. Mastery. Self-control. Subtlety. Flexibility. Dexterity. Craft. Ability to choose one's own action. Determination to see a task through to completion.

REVERSE MEANING: The reverse meaning of this card is weakness of will. Insecurity. Disquiet. Delay. Limited interest. Lack of imagination. The use of one's skill for destructive ends. Will power applied to evil ends.

I
LE BATELEUR
THE MAGICIAN or
THE JUGGLER

II JUNON — THE HIGH PRIESTESS

DESCRIPTION: A stately goddess stands in her bare feet with a tiara on her head and a large rod or staff in her left hand. Behind her stands a golden peacock with colorful feathers suggesting a wide range of beauty and knowledge. She is a tall and broad shouldered woman suggesting challenge to masculine supremacy. She is the end result of knowledge and wisdom, the perfect woman and the essence of all that is female.

DIVINATORY MEANING: This card represents wisdom. Sageness. Common sense. Enlightenment. Knowledge. Education. Penetration. Foresight. Intuition. Understanding. Intelligence. Comprehension.

REVERSE MEANING: The reverse meaning of this card is ignorance. Accepting superficial knowledge. Shortsightedness. Shallowness. Conceit. Selfishness.

II
JUNON — THE HIGH PRIESTESS

III L'IMPERATRICE — THE EMPRESS

DESCRIPTION: A woman, possibly soon to be a mother, sits upon a throne. Her robes are similar to those worn by the emperor and in her right hand she holds a similar kind of scepter. She wears a crown on her head and two strands of pearls around her neck. She stares straight ahead with resolution and stability. She is the symbol of feminine productivity and action.

DIVINATORY MEANING: This card symbolizes feminine progress. Evolution. Attainment. Fruitfulness. Accomplishment. Achievement. Marriage. Material wealth. Fertility.

REVERSE MEANING: The reverse meaning of this card is vacillation. Indecision. Lack of concentration. Inaction. Delay in accomplishment or progress. Anxiety.

III
L'IMPERATRICE — THE EMPRESS

IIII L'EMPEREUR — THE EMPEROR

DESCRIPTION: A regal man of great stature with a beard, mustache and long flowing hair sits upon his throne. Upon his head is a golden crown and in his right hand he holds a scepter. He is adorned with various ornaments. Beside him, beneath his left hand, is a shield of authority and at his waist is the sword of power. Suspended from a ceremonial ribbon around his neck is a golden amulet.

DIVINATORY MEANING: This card represents worldly power. Competence. Proficiency. Skill. Savoir-faire. Leadership. Wealth. Stability. Perseverance. Indomitable spirit. Conviction. Endurance. Domination of intelligence and reason over emotion and passion. Realization of goals.

REVERSE MEANING: The reverse meaning of this card is immaturity. Ineffectiveness. Lack of strength. Feebleness. Inability. Failure to control petty emotions. Weak character.

IIII
L'EMPEREUR — THE EMPEROR

V JUPITER — HIEROPHANT OR POPE

DESCRIPTION: An elderly man wearing a miter holds in his right hand a rod of doctrine. His facial expression suggests patience and kindness. Poised before him is the sacred eagle, symbol of wisdom.

DIVINATORY MEANING: This card symbolizes mercy. Humility. Kindness. Goodness. Forgiveness. Leniency. Indulgence. Compassion. Inspiration. Alliance. A person to whom one has recourse. Ritual. Conformity. Servitude. A religious or spiritual person.

REVERSE MEANING: The reverse meaning of this card is overkindness. Foolish exercise of generosity. Susceptibility. Impotence. Vulnerability. Frailty. Unorthodoxy. Unconventionality. Insensitivity. Renunciation.

V
JUPITER — HIEROPHANT or POPE

VI L'AMOUREUX — THE LOVERS

DESCRIPTION: A young man clasps the hands of a young maiden. Possibly the man and woman represent Adam and Eve. To their right is an elderly man with a cane suggesting vice. Above them is Cupid pointing an arrow of influence and decision. The charm of the young man and woman is suspect by the temptations of the elderly man and the influence of Cupid.

DIVINATORY MEANING: This card suggests the necessity for testing or subjecting to trial. The struggle between sacred and profane love. Putting to the proof. Examining. Speculating. Tempting. Yearning. Possible predicaments. Beauty. Perfection. Compatibility. Harmony. Unanimity. Beginning of a possible romance.

REVERSE MEANING: The reverse meaning of this card is failure when put to the test. Unreliability. Unwise plans. Infidelity. Interference. Fickleness. Untrustworthiness. Inconsistency. The possibility of a wrong choice. Frustrations in love and marriage. Falling into a trap. Separation. Inadequacy to meet and overcome a personal problem.

VI
L'AMOUREUX — THE LOVERS

VII LE CHARIOT — THE CHARIOT

DESCRIPTION: A crowned conqueror stands erect under a canopy between two pillars. He bears a scepter in his gloved left hand. He wears a suit of armor with pointed epaulets suggesting preparation for conflict. Below the conqueror is his triumphal chariot drawn by two spirited horses pulling apart from each other. The two wheels of the chariot represent disturbance and distress. The wheels may also signify the union of negative and positive.

DIVINATORY MEANING: This card suggests trouble and adversity, possibly already overcome. Ordeal. Obstacle. Great effort. Overwhelming odds. Ascendancy. Acclamation. Conquest. Victory. Triumph. Greatness. The determination to mix hard work with times of productive solitude.

REVERSE MEANING: The reverse meaning of this card is to be unsuccessful. Defeat. Failure at the last minute to succeed. Sudden collapse of plans. Conquered. Overwhelmed. Failure to meet responsibility and to face reality.

VII
LE CHARIOT — THE CHARIOT

VIII LA JUSTICE — JUSTICE

DESCRIPTION: The crowned female figure of Justice, one of the cardinal virtues, holds the scales of justice balanced in her left hand suggesting equitableness and fairness. In her right hand she holds a double edged sword, indicating that sometimes action both ways successfully penetrates a difficult situation. She stands resolute and firm in her convictions. She is a pillar of moral strength and integrity, the preservation of kingdoms and the law of order and righteousness.

DIVINATORY MEANING: This card means justice. Fairness. Reasonableness. Moderation. Neutrality. Balance. Sensibility. Poise. Righteousness. Virtue. Integrity. Goodness. Honor. Virginity. Self-satisfaction in accomplishments.

REVERSE MEANING: The reverse meaning of this card is bias. False accusations. Abuse. Bigotry. Severity in judgment. Unfairness. Intolerance. Inequality. Dogmatism. Lack of proper perspective. Lawlessness. Violence.

VIII
LA JUSTICE — JUSTICE

VIIII L'ERMITE—THE HERMIT

DESCRIPTION: An aged, bearded man garbed in a heavy habit with a cowl hanging down from his neck bears in his right hand the lantern of occult science. In his left hand he holds a straight walking stick of magic. His belt is made of knotted rope. He is the guardian of time. He is the wise man seeking wisdom and truth.

DIVINATORY MEANING: This card represents prudence. Discretion. Deliberation. Inner wisdom. Caution. Vigilance. Circumspection. Thriftiness. Self-denial. Withdrawal. Silent counsel. Solicitude. Under certain circumstances this card also represents recession. Regression. Desertion. Annulment.

REVERSE MEANING: The reverse meaning of this card is imprudence. Hastiness. Rashness. Prematurity. Immaturity. Childishness. Lack of patience. Foolish acts. Overprudence resulting in unnecessary delay.

VIIII
L'ERMITE — THE HERMIT

X LA ROUE DE FORTUNE— THE WHEEL OF FORTUNE

DESCRIPTION: The wheel of fortune revolves on its axis of two straight branches springing from the edge of a cliff of barren rock and dirt. Near the wheel of fortune grows a bed of red roses signifying hope. The blindfolded woman of fortune with an expression of blissful unawareness turns the wheel depicting the uncertainty of change. She is the dispenser of sorrow and joy. At the top of the wheel sits a man with his legs crossed in the form of an X while his right hand grasps the hand of a woman. The man holds a hat in his left hand, rejoicing in his deliverance and success. On the descending side of the wheel a man falls off the edge of the cliff. Love and death are thus equally dispensed. The wheel of fortune has eight spokes signifying that each state of life is across the wheel from its opposite. The wheel of fortune is the perpetual motion of a continuously changing universe and the flowing of human life.

DIVINATORY MEANING: This card signifies progress. Advancement for better or possibly worse. Good fortune. Luck. Godsend. Probability. Ultimate infinity. Fate. Destiny. Future. Unexpected events may occur. The entire sequence of the wheel suggests the course of events from beginning to end. Inevitability. Necessity. That which was, is and shall be remains the same so one must be alert to unexpected opportunity.

REVERSE MEANING: The reverse meaning of this card is failure. Ill luck. Without good fortune. A turn for the worse. Unexpected bad fate. Interruption or inconsistency in expected events. Broken sequence.

X
LA ROUE DE FORTUNE—
THE WHEEL OF FORTUNE

XI LA FORCE — STRENGTH

DESCRIPTION: This card depicts a Hercules confidently and successfully restraining a lion with his bare hands. On the ground lies a red club discarded as a sign of great inner strength and self-confidence.

DIVINATORY MEANING: This card symbolizes courage. Fortitude. Energy. Determination. Magnanimity. Resolution. Strength to endure in spite of all obstacles. Physical strength. Spiritual power. Overcoming material power. Hidden forces at work. Self-reliance. Heroism. Virility. Confidence. Intensity. Defiance. Fervor. Zeal. Triumph of love over hate.

REVERSE MEANING: The reverse meaning of this card is weakness. Impotency. Pettiness. Lack of faith. Abuse of power. Tyranny. Overbearingness. Discord. Succumbing to temptation.

XI
LA FORCE — STRENGTH

XII LE PENDU — THE HANGED MAN

DESCRIPTION: A man hangs suspended from a wooden beam between two living tree trunks. His right foot is tied with heavy cord and his hands are bound behind his back. Only one of the man's legs shows below the knee. His face expresses repentance rather than suffering.

DIVINATORY MEANING: This card suggests life in suspension. Reversal of the mind and one's way of life. Transition. Abandonment. Renunciation. The changing of life's forces. Sacrifice. Readjustment. Regeneration. Rebirth. Improvement. Efforts and sacrifices may have to be undertaken to succeed towards a goal which may not be reached.

REVERSE MEANING: The reverse meaning of this card is lack of sacrifice. Unwillingness to make the necessary effort. Failure to give of one's self. Preoccupation with the ego. False prophecy.

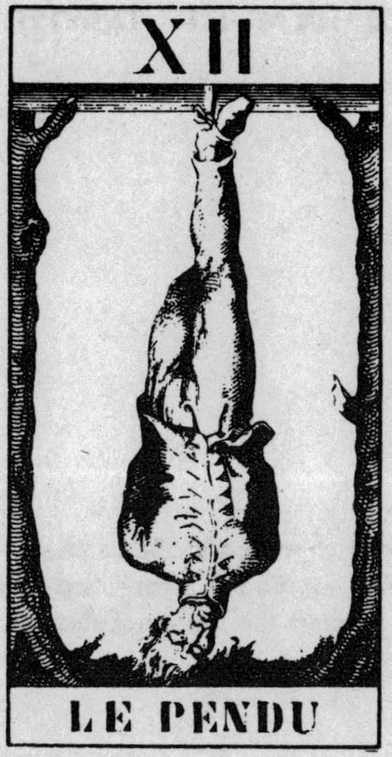

XII
LE PENDU — THE HANGED MAN

XIII LA MORT—DEATH

DESCRIPTION: A skeleton using a scythe stands upon the barren ground to which he has just laid waste. The Death card is the unlucky number thirteen. The skeleton suggests the finality of the past.

DIVINATORY MEANING: This card suggests clearing the way for transformation. Alteration. Sudden change. Great change. Death of the old self, though not necessarily physical death. Loss. Failure. Mishap. Debacle. Disaster. Ruin. End. Death. The ending of a familiar situation or friendship. Loss of income or financial security. Beginning of a new era.

REVERSE MEANING: The reverse meaning of this card is stagnation. Inertia. Partial change. Immobility. Possibly death just escaped or recovery from shock or illness.

XIII
LA MORT — DEATH

XIIII TEMPERANCE — TEMPERANCE

DESCRIPTION: The virtue of temperance is depicted by a winged angel pouring the essence of life from a round urn into a six-sided urn. She stands before the hills of wisdom and understanding. The waterfall symbolizes the flowing of the past through the present into the future. The urns are a feminine symbol of moderation. The pouring of the liquid without spilling its contents symbolizes frugality and discipline.

DIVINATORY MEANING: This card suggests moderation. Temperance. Patience. Self-control. Frugality. Coordination. Accommodation. Reflection. Harmony. The mixing or bringing together into a perfect union. Friendship. Compatibility. Consolidation. Fusion. Putting into successful combination.

REVERSE MEANING: The reverse meaning of this card is discord. Hostility. Disunion. Conflict of interest in business or personal affairs. Inability to work with others. Sterility. Stubbornness. Lack of patience. Desires unfulfilled.

XIIII
TEMPERANCE — TEMPERANCE

XV LE DIABLE — THE DEVIL

DESCRIPTION: A naked devil with wild eyes, hooked nose, horned ears, taloned hands, hooved feet and a long tail stands above a remorseful woman who holds her head in a bowed position with her hands covering her eyes. The devil's right hand is upraised, symbolizing black magic and destruction. In his left hand he holds a two pronged pitchfork. The Devil is the indispensable bearer of death, disaster and misery. Human suffering and desolation begotten by man.

DIVINATORY MEANING: This card suggests bondage. Enslavement. Subordination. Matter over mind. Ravage. Violence. Shock. Fatality. Self-punishment. Disaster. Downfall. Weird experience. Astral influence. Black magic.

REVERSE MEANING: The reverse meaning of this card is release from bondage. Throwing off shackles. Respite. Overcoming insurmountable handicaps. The beginning of spiritual understanding. The realization that much of bondage is surmountable. The first steps towards enlightenment. Overcoming the fear of one's own self.

XV
LE DIABLE — THE DEVIL

XVI LA MAISON DE DIEU —
THE HOUSE OF GOD or
THE LIGHTNING STRUCK TOWER

DESCRIPTION: A tower is struck violently by lightning, possibly originating directly from the sun. Debris, brick, timber and part of the materialistic wall tumble to the ground. One man falls head first from the tower while another man already lies on the ground. The tower of previous concepts breaks down in a lightning flash of truth. The tower is struck and it is now the devil's tower.

DIVINATORY MEANING: This card suggests the breaking down of existing forms to make way for new ones. Sudden and unexpected events. Ruin and misery. Adversity. Downfall. Breakdown. Havoc. Undoing. Major catastrophe. Terrible danger. Evil influences. Loss of stability. A sudden event which destroys trust. Something occurring which upsets old beliefs and notions. A fitful event. Bankruptcy. Loss of money. Loss of security. Setback.

REVERSE MEANING: The reverse meaning of this card is continued oppression. Inability to effect a necessary change. Caught in an untenable situation. Entrapped. Imprisoned. Oppressed.

XVI
LA MAISON DE DIEU
THE HOUSE OF GOD or
THE LIGHTNING STRUCK TOWER

XVII L'ETOILE—THE STAR

DESCRIPTION: A semi-nude young girl pours the waters of life into a large lake signifying the stirring of new ideas and new concepts. Four gold and three red stars are ablaze in color and radiate upon her. The stars of hope ascend above her.

DIVINATORY MEANING: This card depicts hope. Faith. Trust. Inspiration. Good omen. Promising opportunity. Bright future. Optimism. Favorable prospects. Insight. Satisfaction. Spiritual love.

REVERSE MEANING: The reverse meaning of this card is hope unfulfilled. Bad luck. Pessimism. Disappointment. Lack of opportunity. Stubbornness. Harmony of short duration.

XVII
L'ETOILE — THE STAR

XVIII LA LUNE — THE MOON

DESCRIPTION: A man sits with his legs crossed and a dog at his feet. He plays a musical instrument to the pleasure of a woman who stands on a balcony. Below them is a crayfish emblematic of the sign of Cancer and ruled over by the moon. The crayfish is slowly crawling up the balcony towards the girl. The pull of the moon draws upon the man and girl. The moon triumphs over the stars because it is brighter and closer to earth.

DIVINATORY MEANING: This card implies deception. Trickery. Insincerity. Dishonesty. Disillusionment. Double dealing. Deceit. Craftiness. False pretense. The crayfish symbolizes that which comes out of the deep and unknown. Unsuspected. Unforeseen perils. Danger. Scandal. Error. Disgrace. Dishonor. Slander. Libel. Immorality. An insincere personal relationship. Superficiality. False friends. Unknown enemies.

REVERSE MEANING: The reverse meaning of this card means minor deceptions. Trifling mistakes. Overcoming bad temptation. Uneasy contentment gained after paying the necessary price.

XVIII
LA LUNE — THE MOON

XVIIII LE SOLEIL — THE SUN

DESCRIPTION: A huge brilliant sun shines brightly upon a boy and girl sitting on the ground holding a book of knowledge in their laps. The boy clasps the girl around the shoulder signifying happiness and contentment. The sun triumphs over the moon and stars. Its rays shine out and touch upon all the earth.

DIVINATORY MEANING: This card suggests satisfaction. Accomplishment. Contentment. Success. Triumph. Achievement. Favorable relationship. Engagement. Comfort. Pleasure. A good friend. Well being. High spirits. Joy. Rewards through work. Achievements in one's interests and work. Unselfish love. Devotion. A happy marriage. Moderation in life. Pleasure in daily existence. Material wealth.

REVERSE MEANING: The reverse meaning of this card means unhappiness. Loneliness. Clouded future. Possibly a broken engagement or cancelled plans. Triumph delayed but maybe not completely destroyed.

XVIIII
LE SOLEIL — THE SUN

XX LE JUGEMENT — JUDGMENT

DESCRIPTION: The angel Gabriel emerges from the heavens, blowing on his red trumpet. One man and three women draped in loin cloths rise from the earth suggesting revival and reawakening. The day of judgment has arrived. The evaluation of one's efforts and accomplishments may be near at hand.

DIVINATORY MEANING: This card suggests rejuvenation. Rehabilitation. Rebirth. Change of position. Readjustment. Improvement. Development. Promotion.

REVERSE MEANING: The reverse meaning of this card means delay. Postponement. Failure to face facts. Failure to achieve happiness. Separation. Divorce. Indecision. Suspension. Disillusionment. Procrastination.

XX
LE JUGEMENT — JUDGMENT

XXI LE MONDE — THE WORLD

DESCRIPTION: A nude female figure is encircled within a wreath of colorful leaves and buds. She represents nature and the divine presence therein. In her hands she clasps a flowing veil or cloth. Above her an eagle spreads its wings symbolizing attainment. Two other eagles support the wreath. Below the female figure are a lion and a bull, guardians of the truth. All that has taken place before culminates now in ultimate completion.

DIVINATORY MEANING: This card represents attainment. Ultimate change. Completion. Perfection. Success. Admiration of others. Culmination. Conclusion. Triumph in undertakings. The final goal to which all other cards have led.

REVERSE MEANING: The reverse meaning of this card is imperfection. Quitting in the middle. Failure to finish what one starts. Refusal to recognize the meanings revealed in the other cards. Lack of vision.

XXI
LE MONDE — THE WORLD

CHAPTER III — SPREADING THE MAJOR ARCANA CARDS

The various known methods of spreading the twenty-two Major Arcana cards are numerous and some of them are exceedingly complicated. One of the earliest and most effective methods is offered here. After several practice spreadings and interpretations this method will become quite natural and easy to use.

The fifty-six Lesser Arcana cards are set aside. The Diviner or Reader of the deck places the twenty-two Major Arcana cards in numerical sequence. The unnumbered card called LE MAT (The Fool) is placed either at the beginning of the deck, in the middle of the deck, between the twentieth and twenty-first numbered card or at the very end of the deck.

The person seeking an answer to a question is known as the Questioner. The Questioner sits at a table opposite the Diviner and both persons maintain a serious mental attitude. The Questioner puts all other thoughts and desires from his mind except the specific question which he states out loud to the Diviner while simultaneously shuffling the deck face down. The person who handles the cards impregnates them with his own personal magnetism and thereby creates a rapport between the subconscious and the cards. The cards may be shuffled either hand over hand or by riffling (separating the deck into two parts and riffling with the thumb so the cards intermix). The shuffling must be done by the person who wishes to have an interpretation or prediction concerning himself or a topic of interest to him, and not by the Diviner, Reader or Interpreter. When the Questioner is satisfied with his shuffling, he places the deck face down in front of the Diviner. The cards are always viewed from the Diviner's position. Beginning with the top card as number one, the second card as number two, and so on, the Diviner turns up the first six cards and places them face up on the table in the sequence shown in the diagram on the following page.

The Diviner must turn the cards over from left to right thereby assuring that the cards continue to point in the same direction as placed on the table by the Questioner. The cards which face the Diviner are said to be positioned for a strong, positive reading and the cards which face the Questioner are said to be upside down or inverted and therefore, have a weak, delayed or even reversed meaning. In the event the first card turned over by the Diviner is reversed or upside down, then the Diviner must turn over the remaining nine cards from the bottom to the top in such a manner as to reverse the direction of each of the cards.

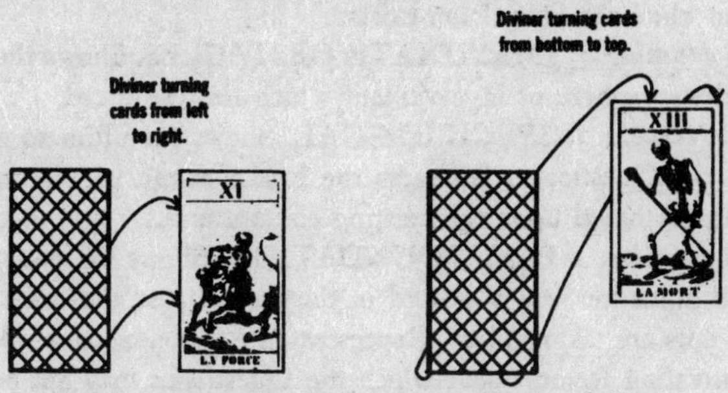

The sequence of laying out the cards is as follows:

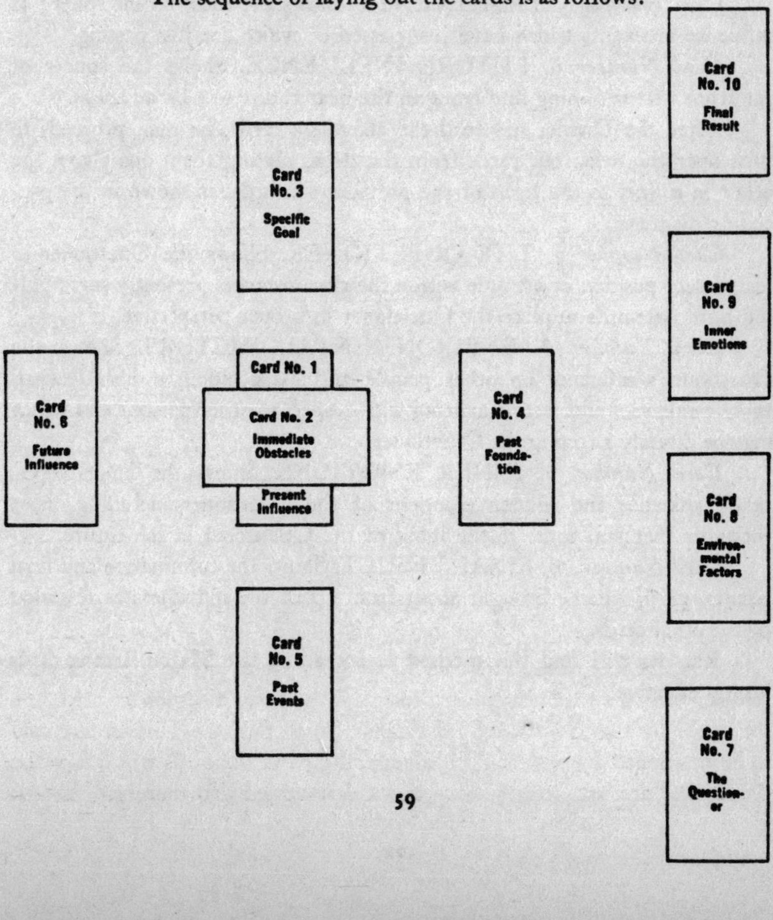

Card Number 1. PRESENT INFLUENCE. Atmosphere in which the Questioner is presently working and living. Shows the area of present influence in which the Questioner exists.

Card Number 2. IMMEDIATE OBSTACLES. Shows the nature of the obstacles or sphere of involvement which lie just ahead.

Card Number 3. SPECIFIC GOAL. Shows the ultimate goal or objective of the Questioner. Indicates the best that can be accomplished by the Questioner based upon the existing circumstances.

Card Number 4. PAST FOUNDATION. Shows the broad and basic events and influences which existed in the distant past and upon which the present events are taking place. Represents the unconscious mind and those subtle motivating factors about which the Questioner may not be aware.

Card Number 5. PAST EVENTS. Shows the most recent sphere of influence or events which have just passed or which are just passing.

Card Number 6. FUTURE INFLUENCE. Shows the sphere of influence that is coming into being in the near future in a broad sense.

After the Diviner has read the above six cards, he then proceeds to turn over the next four cards from the deck, placing them one above the other in a line, to the right of the previous six cards, as shown in the preceding diagram.

Card Number 7. THE QUESTIONER. Shows the Questioner in his present position or attitude within the circumstances presently surrounding him. Attempts to place the Questioner in proper perspective.

Card Number 8. ENVIRONMENTAL FACTORS. Shows the Questioner's influence on other people and his position in life. Reveals those tendencies and factors existing with respect to other persons and which may be directly affecting the Questioner.

Card Number 9. INNER EMOTIONS. Shows the inner hopes, fears, anxieties and hidden emotions of the Questioner including those thoughts that will come to the mind of the Questioner in the future.

Card Number 10. FINAL RESULT. Shows the culmination and final results which will be brought about from all of the influences as revealed by the other cards.

Readers will find this method of spreading the Major Arcana cards highly effective.

CHAPTER IV — THE LESSER ARCANA CARDS

The fifty-six Lesser Arcana or Minor Arcana cards of the Tarot 1JJ deck are divided equally into four suits containing fourteen cards each suit, corresponding to the suits in an ordinary deck of cards.

> The epees or swords correspond to spades. This suit is associated with strength, strife and misfortune. Spades are identified with fire.
>
> The batons or scepters correspond to clubs. This suit is associated with enterprise and glory. Clubs are identified with air.
>
> The coupes or cups correspond to hearts. This suit is associated with love and happiness. Hearts are identified with water.
>
> The deniers or coins correspond to diamonds. This suit is associated with money and interest. Diamonds are identified with earth.

Within each suit there are nine cards numbered X to II plus an Ace and also four dress cards: King, Queen, Cavalier and Page.

The fifty-six Lesser Arcana cards in each suit with suggested divinatory meanings and reverse meanings are as follows:

THE EPEES OR SWORDS
(Correspond to Spades)

Swords generally represent courage, boldness, force, strength, authority, aggression and ambition. These cards represent activity, progress and accomplishment for good or bad.

ROI DES EPEES
The King of Epees

DESCRIPTION: The King of Epees with stern face and erect posture sits on his throne resplendent in full armor. He represents power, authority and the law. He holds upright in his right hand the sword of his authority and the sign (sword) of his suit.

DIVINATORY MEANING: This card symbolizes an active and determined man. Experienced. Authoritative. Controlled. Commanding. A professional man. Highly analytical. Justice. Force. Power. Superiority.

REVERSE MEANING: The reverse meaning of this card is a person who may pursue a matter to ruin. Cruelty. Conflict. Selfishness. A sadist. A dangerous person. A wicked person.

REINE DES EPEES
The Queen of Epees

DESCRIPTION: The Queen of Epees is resplendent in beautiful robes. She stands with upraised sword. Her left hand is raised as if to signify recognition or generosity. She is one who has suffered a great loss.

DIVINATORY MEANING: This card means a sharp, quick-witted, keen person. Possibly the bearer of evil or slanderous words. May signify a widow or woman of sadness. Mourning. Privation. Loneliness. Separation.

REVERSE MEANING: The reverse meaning of this card is narrow-mindedness. Maliciousness. Bigotry. Deceitfulness. Vengefulness. Prudishness. A treacherous enemy.

CHEVALIER DES EPEES
The Cavalier of Epees

DESCRIPTION: The Cavalier of Epees sits upon his rearing horse and brandishes his sword. He wears a plumed hat and flowing red cape. He is the defender of good and the opponent of evil. He symbolizes chivalry and bravery. He is good at heart and courageous. He is the forerunner of activity. His traits include a shrewdness which is difficult to perceive.

DIVINATORY MEANING: This card symbolizes bravery. Skill. Capacity. The strength and dash of a young man. Heroic action. Opposition and war. The headlong rush into the unknown without fear. The surrounding cards will indicate the influences around the Cavalier in his gallant pursuit.

REVERSE MEANING: The reverse meaning of this card is incapacity. Imprudence. Dispute or ruin over a woman. Impulsive mistakes. Conceited fool.

VALET DES EPEES
The Page of Epees

DESCRIPTION: A light-footed page with plumed hat stands firmly on the ground with sword in his right hand.

DIVINATORY MEANING: This card symbolizes a person adept at perceiving, discerning and uncovering the unknown or less obvious. He has the quality of perception. Vigilance. Agility. Spying.

REVERSE MEANING: The reverse meaning of this card is to be revealed as an imposter. Unprepared state. Unforeseen. Illness is also possible. Powerless in the face of stronger forces.

TEN OF EPEES

DIVINATORY MEANING: Pain. Affliction. Sadness. Mental anguish. Trouble. Misfortune. Ruin. Disappointment.

REVERSE MEANING: Benefit. Advantage. Profit. Temporary gain. Improvement. Passing success.

NINE OF EPEES

DIVINATORY MEANING: Misery. Concern. Quarrel. Unhappiness. Miscarriage. Anxiety over a loved one.

REVERSE MEANING: Doubt. Suspicion. Slanderous gossip.

EIGHT OF EPEES

DIVINATORY MEANING: Crisis. Calamity. Conflict. Domination. Imprisonment. Turmoil. Bad news. Criticism.

REVERSE MEANING: Treachery in the past. Regeneration. Rebirth. New beginnings. Hard work. Overcoming depressed state of mind.

SEVEN OF EPEES

DIVINATORY MEANING: New plans. Wishes about to be fulfilled. Attempt. Endeavor. Hope. Confidence.

REVERSE MEANING: Arguments. Quarrels. Uncertain counsel or advice.

SIX OF EPEES

DIVINATORY MEANING: A trip or journey. Voyage. Attempt through difficulties.

REVERSE MEANING: Stalemate. Unwanted proposal. No immediate solution to present difficulties.

FIVE OF EPEES

DIVINATORY MEANING: Conquest. Destruction of others. Degradation. Adversaries may arise.

REVERSE MEANING: Uncertain outlook. Chance of loss or defeat. Weakness. Possible misfortune befalling a friend.

FOUR OF EPEES

DIVINATORY MEANING: Respite. Rest. Replenishment. Solitude. Exile. Retreat. Temporary seclusion.

REVERSE MEANING: Activity. Circumspection. Precaution. Economy. Guarded advancement. Desire to recover what is lost.

THREE OF EPEES

DIVINATORY MEANING: Absence. Sorrow. Strife. Removal. Dispersion.

REVERSE MEANING: Distraction. Confusion. Disorder. Error. Incompatibility. Separation.

TWO OF EPEES

DIVINATORY MEANING: Stalemate. Offsetting factors. Balance. Harmony. Firmness.

REVERSE MEANING: Duplicity. Falsehood. Misrepresentation. Disloyalty. Dishonor. Treachery.

ACE OF EPEES

DESCRIPTION: A hand firmly holds the great sword which is encircled by the crown of authority. On either side of the sword grow leaves and buds of many colors signifying progress and advancement.

DIVINATORY MEANING: Great determination. Strength. Force. Excessiveness. Triumph. Power. Success. Prosperity.

REVERSE MEANING: Debacle. Tyranny. Disaster. Self-destruction. Violent temper. Embarrassment. Obstacle.

THE BATONS OR SCEPTERS
(Correspond to Clubs)

Batons generally represent enterprise and growth. Progress. Advancement. Animation. Enterprise. These cards also represent modest and humble persons.

ROI DE BATON
The King of Batons

DESCRIPTION: The King of Batons is more noble and elderly than the King of Spades. He sits upon his throne wearing the crown of his authority and holding in his right hand the sign (scepter) of his suit. He is loyal and devoted.

DIVINATORY MEANING: This card means an honest and conscientious person. Mature. Wise. Devoted. Friendly. Sympathetic. Educated.

REVERSE MEANING: The reverse meaning of this card is severity. Austerity. Somewhat excessive and exaggerated ideas. Dogmatic.

REINE DE BATON
The Queen of Batons

DESCRIPTION: The Queen of Batons is dressed in beautiful robes and holds a large scepter in her right hand and a small scepter in her left hand. She is a practical person with good common sense.

DIVINATORY MEANING: This card means a sympathetic and understanding person. Friendly. Loving. Honorable. Chaste. Practical. Full of feminine charm and grace.

REVERSE MEANING: The reverse meaning of this card is jealousy. Deceit. Possible infidelity. Unstable emotions. Fickleness.

CHEVALIER DES BATONS
The Cavalier of Batons

DESCRIPTION: The Cavalier of Batons rears his horse and raises his menacing club in preparation for charging or advancing. He is in a hurry and he indicates change.

DIVINATORY MEANING: This card symbolizes departure. Journey. Advancement into the unknown. Alteration. Flight. Absence.

REVERSE MEANING: The reverse meaning of this card is discord. Interruption. Unexpected change. Quarreling. Breakup of personal relationships.

VALET DE BATON
The Page of Batons

DESCRIPTION: A thin page stands in a pose of acquiescence. He holds his plumed hat in his left hand and a scepter in his right hand. He may be a messenger or bearer of unusual news.

DIVINATORY MEANING: This card symbolizes a faithful and loyal person. An envoy. Emissary. Entrusted friend. A stranger with good intentions.

REVERSE MEANING: The reverse meaning of this card is indecision in proceeding. Reluctance. Instability. Unable to make decisions. A gossip. Bearer of bad tidings. Displeasure.

TEN OF BATONS

DIVINATORY MEANING: Overburdened. Excessive pressures. Problems soon to be resolved. Striving to meet a goal or to maintain a certain level or position.

REVERSE MEANING: Difficulties. Intrigues. Duplicity. Treachery. A Traitor. Deceiver. Subterfuge.

NINE OF BATONS

DIVINATORY MEANING: Expectation of difficulties and changes. Awaiting tribulation. Hidden enemies. Discipline.

REVERSE MEANING: Obstacles. Adversity. Problems. Delays. Displeasure. Calamity. Disaster.

EIGHT OF BATONS

DIVINATORY MEANING: Swift activity. Sudden progress or movement. Speed. Hastily made decisions.

REVERSE MEANING: Thorns of dispute. Jealousy. Harassment. Quarrels. Action without thought. Discord.

SEVEN OF BATONS

DIVINATORY MEANING: Success. Gain. Overcoming obstacles and challenges. Surmounting overwhelming odds. Advantage.

REVERSE MEANING: Consternation. Anxiety. Embarrassment. Indecision. Hesitancy causing losses. Uncertainty.

SIX OF BATONS

DIVINATORY MEANING: Conquest. Triumph. Good news. Gain. Advancement. Expectation.

REVERSE MEANING: Indefinite delay. Fear. Apprehension. Disloyalty.

FIVE OF BATONS

DIVINATORY MEANING: Unsatisfied desires. Struggle. Labor. Endeavors.

REVERSE MEANING: Trickery. Contradictions. Complexity. Involvement. Possible law suit.

FOUR OF BATONS

DIVINATORY MEANING: Romance. Society. Harmony. Newly acquired prosperity. Peace. Tranquility.

REVERSE MEANING: Loss of full tranquility. Unfulfilled romance. Insecurity.

THREE OF BATONS

DIVINATORY MEANING: Practical knowledge. Business acumen. Strength. Enterprise. Negotiations.

REVERSE MEANING: Assistance with an ulterior motive. Treachery. Rejection. Loss.

TWO OF BATONS

DIVINATORY MEANING: Mature individual. Ruler. Attainment of goals and needs.

REVERSE MEANING: Sadness. Trouble. Restraint caused by others. Loss of faith.

ACE OF BATONS

DESCRIPTION: The hand of Life firmly holds a large flowering club from which spring many branches and leaves signifying fertility and progress.

DIVINATORY MEANING: Creation. Beginning. Birth. Invention. Start of an undertaking. Fortune. Enterprise. Gain. Inheritance.

REVERSE MEANING: False start. Cloudy outlook. Unrealized goal. Decadence. Empty existence. Vexation.

THE COUPES OR CUPS
(Correspond to Hearts)

Coupes generally represent love, happiness, gaiety and joy. The cups hold water which is a symbol of pleasure and happiness. These cards represent passions and deep feelings.

ROI DE COUPE
The King of Coupes

DESCRIPTION: The King of Coupes holds a small scepter in his left hand and a great cup in his right. He is kind and considerate. He is level-headed and responsible.

DIVINATORY MEANING: This card means a man of responsibility and creativity. Learned person. Professional. Businessman. Lawyer. Artist. Religious person. Scientist. A considerate person. Kindly. Reliable. Responsible.

REVERSE MEANING: The reverse meaning of this card is artistic temperament. Double-dealing. Dishonesty. Scandal. Loss. Ruin. Injustice.

REINE DES COUPES
The Queen of Coupes

DESCRIPTION: The Queen of Coupes similar to the King holds a scepter in her left hand and in her other hand a great cup. She is a loving, devoted and practical person.

DIVINATORY MEANING: This card means a warm-hearted and fair person. Beloved. Adored. Good friend and mother. Devoted wife. Practical. Honest.

REVERSE MEANING: The reverse meaning of this card is inconsistency of honor. Possible immorality. Dishonesty. Unreliability.

CHEVALIER DES COUPES
The Cavalier of Coupes

DESCRIPTION: The Cavalier of Coupes rides gracefully on his horse. He holds a great cup in his right hand and appears contemplative.

DIVINATORY MEANING: This card means an invitation or opportunity may soon arise. Attraction. Inducement. Appeal. Request. Challenge. Proposal.

REVERSE MEANING: The reverse meaning of this card is subtlety. Artifice. Trickery. Deception. Fraud. A sly and cunning person.

VALET DE COUPE
The Page of Coupes

DECRIPTION: A somewhat studious and serious page holds a great cup upraised before him. He is a loyal and helpful person.

DIVINATORY MEANING: This card symbolizes a studious and intent person. Reflective. Meditative. Loyal. Willing to offer services and efforts towards a specific goal.

REVERSE MEANING: The reverse meaning of this card is inclination. Deviation. Susceptibility. Temporary distraction.

TEN OF COUPES

DIVINATORY MEANING: Happiness. Joy. Pleasure. Peace. Love. Contentment. Good family life.

REVERSE MEANING. Loss of friendship. Unhappiness. Family quarrel. Pettiness. Rage.

NINE OF COUPES

DIVINATORY MEANING: Success. Material attainment. Well-being. Abundance. Good health.

REVERSE MEANING: Mistakes. Material loss. Imperfections. Misplaced truth. False freedom.

EIGHT OF COUPES

DIVINATORY MEANING: Discontinuance of effort. Disappointment. Abandonment of previous plans. Shyness. Modesty.

REVERSE MEANING: Happiness. Effort continued until full success is attained.

SEVEN OF COUPES

DIVINATORY MEANING: Fantasy. Unrealistic attitudes. Imagination. Daydreams. Foolish whims.

REVERSE MEANING: Desire. Determination. Strong will power. A goal nearly attained.

SIX OF COUPES

DIVINATORY MEANING: Memories. Past influences. Things that have vanished. Childhood passed. Nostalgia.

REVERSE MEANING: The future. Opportunities ahead. Coming events. New vistas. Plans that may fail.

FIVE OF COUPES

DIVINATORY MEANING: Partial loss. Regret. Friendship without real meaning. Marriage without real love. Imperfection. Flaw. Inheritance.

REVERSE MEANING: Hopeful outlook. Favorable expectations. New alliances.

FOUR OF COUPES

DIVINATORY MEANING: Weariness. Aversion. Disgust. Disappointment. Unhappiness. Bitter experience.

REVERSE MEANING: New possibilities. New relationships. New approaches to old problems.

THREE OF COUPES

DIVINATORY MEANING: Resolution of a problem. Conclusion. Fulfillment. Solace. Healing.

REVERSE MEANING: Excessive pleasures. Overabundance. Superfluity. Loss of prestige. Delays.

TWO OF COUPES

DIVINATORY MEANING: Love. Friendship beginning or renewed. Passion. Union. Engagement. Cooperation. Partnership. Marriage.

REVERSE MEANING: Unsatisfactory love. False friendship. Troubled relationship. Divorce. Separation.

ACE OF COUPES

DESCRIPTION: A large ornate cup signifies the holding of great abundance. This card is the ultimate of love and happiness.

DIVINATORY MEANING: Great abundance. Fulfillment. Perfection. Joy. Fertility. Opulence. Fullness. Happiness.

REVERSE MEANING: Change. Alteration. Erosion. Instability. Sterility. Unrequited love.

THE DENIERS OR COINS
(Correspond to Diamonds)

Deniers generally represent material and financial matters. This may take the form of money, occupation, material gain, business development, etc. These cards represent deep sensitivity and involvement.

ROI DE DENIER
The King of Deniers

DESCRIPTION: The King of Deniers sits upon his throne and holds aloft a great coin, sign of his suit. His expression is that of an experienced, capable and prosperous person.

DIVINATORY MEANING: This card means an experienced and successful leader. A person of character and intelligence. Business acumen. Mathematical ability. Loyal friend.

REVERSE MEANING: The reverse meaning of this card is corruption. Using any means to achieve the desired end. Vice. Avarice. Unfaithfulness.

REINE DE DENIER
The Queen of Deniers

DESCRIPTION: The Queen of Deniers holds aloft the great coin. Her face expresses intelligence, awareness and generosity.

DIVINATORY MEANING: This card means prosperity and well-being. Wealth. Abundance. Luxury. Extreme comfort. Generosity. Security. Liberty. Magnificance. Grace. Dignity.

REVERSE MEANING: The reverse meaning of this card is false prosperity. Suspense. Suspicion. Responsibilities neglected. Vicious person. Untrusting person.

CHEVALIER DES DENIERS
The Cavalier of Deniers

DESCRIPTION: The Cavalier of Deniers sits majestically upon his horse with sword in hand and the great coin above him. Both the Cavalier and his horse express confidence and accomplishment.

DIVINATORY MEANING: This card means a mature and responsible person. Reliable. Methodical. Patient. Persistent. Ability to conclude a task.

REVERSE MEANING: The reverse meaning of this card is stagnation. Carelessness. Inertia. Lack of determination or direction. Narrow-mindedness. Limited by dogmatic views.

VALET DE DENIER
The Page of Deniers

DESCRIPTION: An articulate page holds the great coin before him. He stares fixedly at the upraised coin as if he is dreaming and unaware of that which is about him.

DIVINATORY MEANING: This card means deep concentration and application. Study. Scholarship. Reflection. Respect for knowledge. Desire for learning and new ideas.

REVERSE MEANING: The reverse meaning of this card is an unrealistic person. Failure to recognize obvious facts. Dissipation of ideas. Illogical thinking. Rebelliousness.

TEN OF DENIERS

DIVINATORY MEANING: Prosperity. Riches. Security. Safety.

REVERSE MEANING: Poor risk. Bad odds. Possible loss. Hazard.

NINE OF DENIERS

DIVINATORY MEANING: Accomplishment. Discernment. Foresight. Safety. Prudence. Material well-being.

REVERSE MEANING: Threat to safety. Roguery. Dissipation. Danger. Storms.

EIGHT OF DENIERS

DIVINATORY MEANING: Apprenticeship. Preliminary learning. Craftsmanship.

REVERSE MEANING: Lack of ambition. Vanity. Conceit. Disillusionment.

SEVEN OF DENIERS

DIVINATORY MEANING: Ingenuity. Growth. Hard work. Progress. Successful dealings.

REVERSE MEANING: Anxiety. Impatience. Uneasiness. Imprudent actions.

SIX OF DENIERS

DIVINATORY MEANING: Generosity. Philanthropy. Charity. Kindness.

REVERSE MEANING: Avarice. Selfishness. Envy. Jealousy. Ungiving of one's self.

FIVE OF DENIERS

DIVINATORY MEANING: Material trouble. Destitution. Loss. Failure. Error. Impoverishment.

REVERSE MEANING: Reversal of bad trend. New interest in matters. Overcoming ruin.

FOUR OF DENIERS

DIVINATORY MEANING: Love of material wealth. Hoarder. Usurer. Skinflint. Miser.

REVERSE MEANING: Setbacks in material holdings. Obstacles. Opposition to further gain. Suspense and delay.

THREE OF DENIERS

DIVINATORY MEANING: Great skill in trade or work. Mastery. Perfection. Artistic ability.

REVERSE MEANING: Sloppiness. Mediocrity. Lower quality. Money problems.

TWO OF DENIERS

DIVINATORY MEANING: Difficulty in launching new projects. Difficult situations arising. New troubles.

REVERSE MEANING: Literary ability. Agility in handling matters. Simulated enjoyment. Enforced gaiety.

ACE OF DENIERS

DESCRIPTION: A large coin signifies very favorable outlook and prosperity.

DIVINATORY MEANING: Perfection. Attainment. Prosperity. Felicity. Great wealth. Riches. Bliss. Ecstasy. Gold. Valuable coins or artifacts. Treasures.

REVERSE MEANING: Prosperity without happiness. Misused wealth. Wasted moneys. Corruption by money.

CHAPTER V —
SPREADING THE 78-CARD DECK

As previously suggested, many followers of tarot find the 22 Major Arcana cards adequate for fortune telling. However, persons well versed in the art of tarot may wish to utilize the full 78-card deck.

Several spreads utilizing the full deck are demonstrated in this section, all of which can be quickly mastered by the Diviner after a little practice.

A—THE TEN CARD SPREAD

This card spread described previously under Chapter III is also applicable when using the entire 78-card deck. The only difference is that before the Questioner shuffles the deck the Diviner should arrange the deck in the following sequence:

> Diamond suit Ace to King, Heart suit Ace to King, Club suit Ace to King, Spade suit Ace to King and the 22 Major Arcana cards No. I Le Bateleur to No. XXI Le Monde. Le Mat is placed either before Le Bateleur; anywhere in the middle of the Major Arcana cards; between Le Jugement and Le Monde; or after Le Monde. Thus when the deck is ready for shuffling by the Questioner the top card face down is either Le Monde or Le Mat.

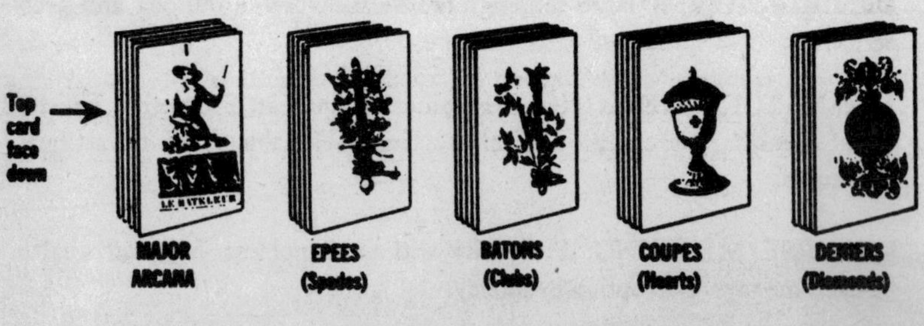

B—THE SEVEN CARD SPREAD

This card spread is especially useful for a *yes* or *no* question. If four or more cards are inverted then the answer is usually no, or little likelihood of a yes, or a delayed yes.

The Diviner separates the 22 Major Arcana cards from the 56 Lesser Arcana cards. The Questioner shuffles the 56 Lesser Arcana cards and deals out the top 11 cards face down on top of the pile of 22 Major Arcana cards. The remaining 45 Lesser Arcana cards are set aside.

The Questioner reshuffles the new pile of 33 cards (11 Lesser Arcana and 22 Major Arcana) while repeating aloud the question to be answered.

The Diviner then deals out the top 7 cards face up from left to right in the following spread:

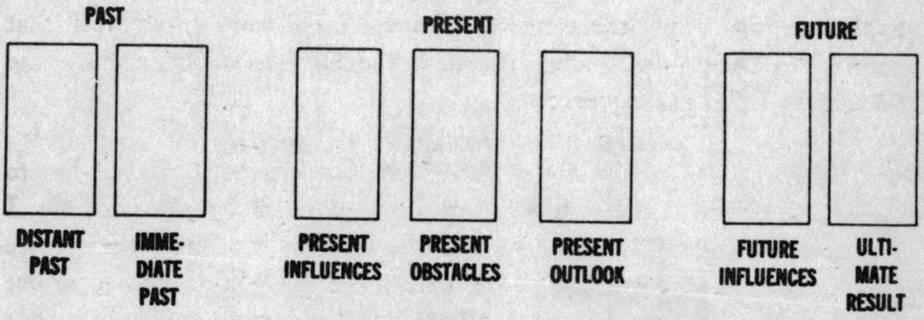

The Diviner reads the cards, stimulated by the symbolic pictures and aided by the divinatory meanings for each card. The rules previously described for the spreading of the Major Arcana cards also apply here. Inverted cards are either weakened, delayed or reversed in meaning. If the first card is inverted then the Diviner, instead of turning over each card from left to right, turns over the remaining top six cards from top to bottom.

C—THE NAME SPREAD

This spread utilizes that important aspect of an individual with which he has been associated and known since birth, his full name. The Name Spread utilizes the full 78-card deck.

After the Questioner shuffles the cards while simultaneously stating his question aloud, the Diviner spreads the cards face up in the same number as the full name of the Questioner.

For example, if the Questioner's full name comprising twenty-one letters is ROBERT EDWIN SOUTHWORTH, the Diviner spreads the first twenty-one cards in three rows from left to right as follows:

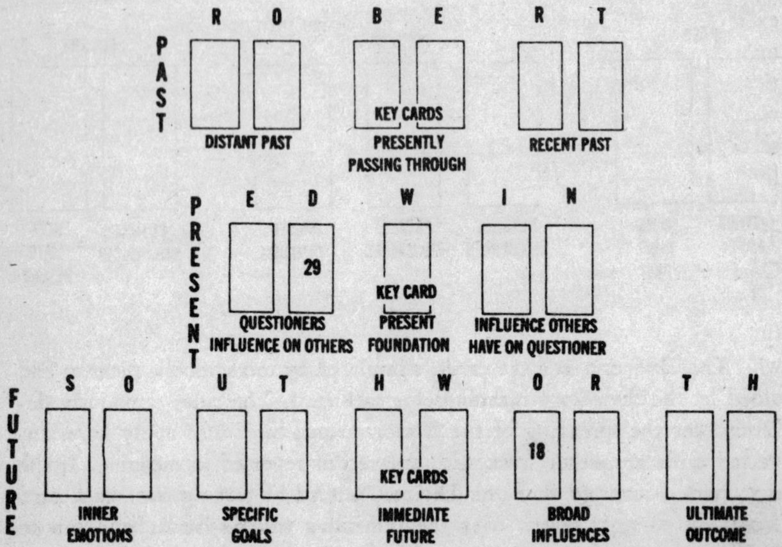

If the Questioner does not have a middle name, then the number of cards in the first row are repeated in the middle row. If the Questioner's name does not contain a minimum of three letters in each of the first and middle names or a minimum of five letters in the last name, then the rows are spread with three, three and five cards representing the first, middle and last names respectively. The center card in each row (or two cards if the row is even numbered) is the *Key* card.

The top row represents the past influences and experiences which the Questioner has experienced. To the left of the center *Key* card are those influences from the distant past which represent the previous broad background of the Questioner. To the right of the *Key* card are those influences which the Questioner has passed through during the relatively recent past, possibly during the past days, weeks or months. The *Key* card in the center represents those influences which the Questioner most recently passed through or may be just completing the passing through.

The middle row of cards represents the period of present influences. To the left of the *Key* card are those influences which the Questioner exerts upon other people with whom he comes into contact. The cards also may show the impressions and opinions held by others about the Questioner. To the right of the *Key* card are those influences and pressures which other people exert upon the Questioner. The center *Key* card represents the foundation and environment in which the Questioner is presently living and working.

The bottom row of cards relates to the future and ultimate outcome. To the left of the *Key* card are the inner emotions and specific goals of the Questioner. To the immediate right of the *Key* card are the broad future influences or spheres of influence that are coming into being in the near future. To the extreme right are the ultimate outcome and final results which will be brought about from all of the influences as revealed by the other cards. The *Key* card represents the immediate future in which the Questioner is presently entering. This card may represent obstacles which will have to be met and overcome or it could represent opportunity, good fortune or progress towards a goal that the Questioner is seeking to attain.

The Name Spread has one additional interesting feature, the *age card*. The age of the Questioner is used to determine the *age card* which has strong meaning. For example, if the Questioner is 18 years of age, then the Diviner counts eighteen cards from left to right beginning at the top row, and the *age card* is found on the bottom row, seventh card from the left. If the Questioner is 29 years of age, then the *age card* is the second card in the second row. The *age card* usually is a very strong and influential card. Its meaning generally is very important and a significant key to the past, present, or future of the Questioner.

D—THE 56 CARD HORSESHOE SPREAD

The full pack of seventy-eight cards is shuffled face down by the Questioner. The Diviner then deals out the first card face down to his right on a part of the table designated pile A and two cards face down on a part of the table designated pile B. The Diviner continues to deal out the deck face down at the rate of one card on pile A and two cards on pile B, one card on pile A, and two cards on pile B, until the entire deck is dealt out, leaving two piles consisting of twenty-six cards in pile A and fifty-two cards in pile B.

Pile A remains where it is for the moment. Pile B is picked up by the Diviner and dealt face down into two new piles designated C and D at the rate of one card on pile C and two cards on pile D, one card on pile C and two cards on pile D, until the full 52 cards are dealt out thus leaving three piles: A=26 cards, C=18 cards and D=34 cards.

The Diviner takes up pile D containing 34 cards and deals face down two new piles designated E and F at the rate of one card on pile E and two cards on pile F, one card on pile E and two cards on pile F, until the full 35 cards are dealt out thus leaving four piles: A=26 cards, C=18 cards, E=12 cards and F=22 cards.

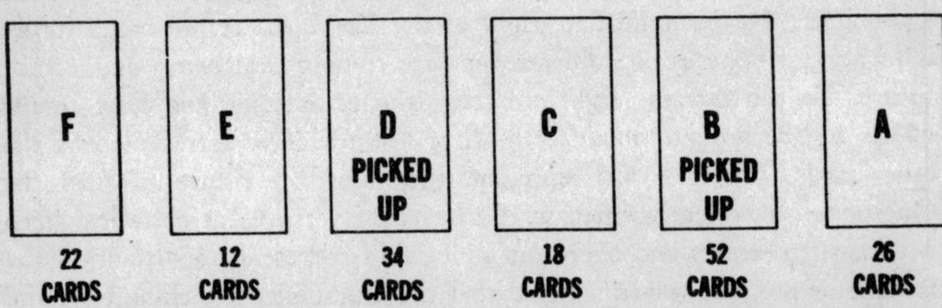

The Diviner puts pile F aside as these 22 cards are not to be used for reading. Pile A is picked up and the Diviner deals out the 26 cards face up from *right* to *left* in the shape of a horseshoe, the first card being at the lowest right-hand corner of the horseshoe, and the twenty-sixth card being at the lowest left-hand corner.

The Diviner reads the cards from *right* to *left* in a connected manner. When this is completed, the Diviner reads the first and twenty-sixth cards together, the second and twenty-fifth cards together, etc., and so on until all the pairs have been read.

After completing the above reading pile A is put aside and pile C is spread out and read exactly in the same way, and then pile E last.

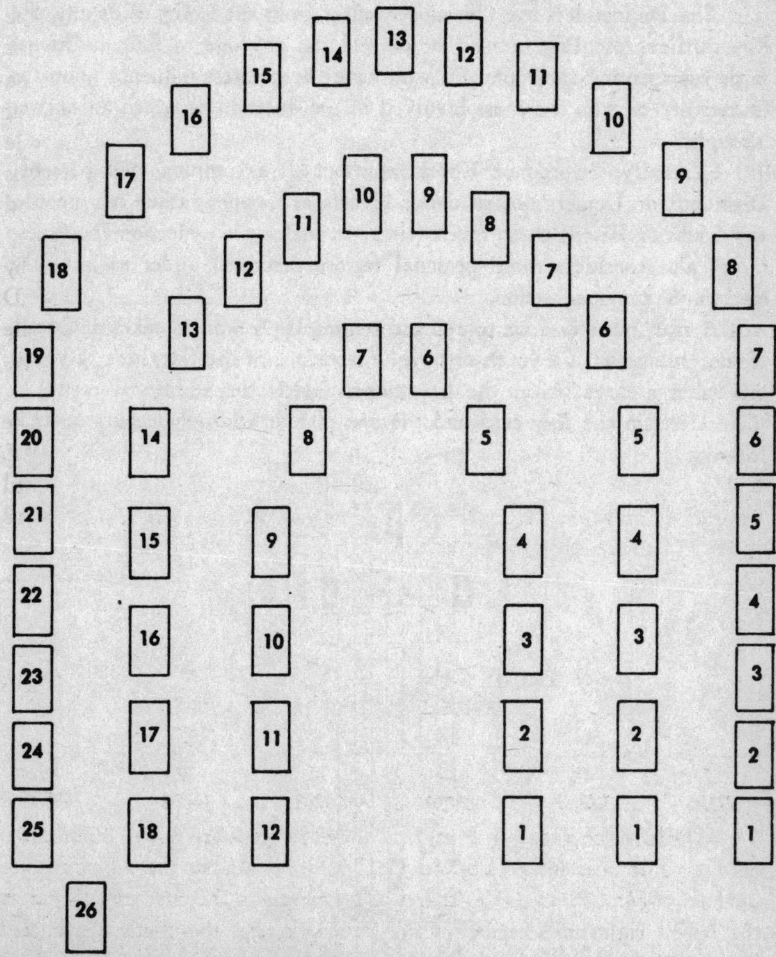

E—THE 54 CARD ROYAL SPREAD

This spread involves the 22 Major Arcana cards, the 16 Court cards (King, Queen, Cavalier and Page) the four Aces and cards II, III and IIII in each suit.

To prepare this spread, the Diviner first removes the 24 cards comprising Roman numerals X through V in each of the four suits.

The Diviner lets the Questioner select from the Court cards any one *Key* card representing himself or herself and any one to four additional cards representing those persons who have the greatest influence upon the Questioner or who are most involved in the question to which an answer is sought.

Generally, Swords or Epees represent dark complexioned persons; Diamonds or Deniers not so dark; Hearts or Coupes rather fair people, and Clubs or Batons those much fairer. In making his selection the Questioner also considers those personal factors described under each of the cards in the previous section.

A man takes a King to represent himself. A woman takes a Queen. If the Questioner is a youth or boy, he takes one of the Cavaliers; a young girl takes a Page. After the Questioner selects the additional cards, he places face up the *Key* card and the one to four additional court cards as follows:

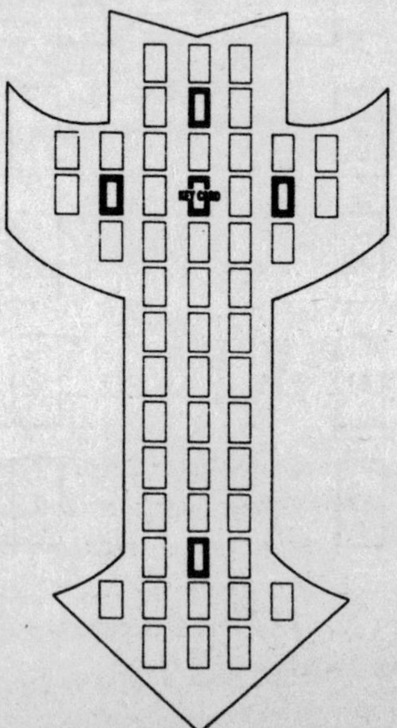

The Questioner then shuffles the remaining cards and the Diviner places the cards face up (either 53 to 50 cards depending upon whether the Questioner placed one to four cards on the table) beginning at the top row from right to left. The Diviner proceeds to read the cards, combining groups of cards to form a series or sequence of events.

F—THE SEVENTH CARD SPREAD

The Questioner removes from the full deck one Court card (King, Queen, Cavalier, or Page) representing himself and places this Key card on the table face upwards, leaving room to the left for seven more cards.

The Questioner shuffles the cards face down and hands the pack to the Diviner who places the top card face up to the left of the *Key* card, then the seventh card from the pack, the fourteenth card from it, the twenty-first card, and so on, until the Diviner has drawn a total of twenty-one cards by taking every seventh card. While dealing the cards the Diviner returns the unused cards to the bottom of the bottom of the pack. The twenty-one cards are arranged in three rows of seven cards each, from *right* to *left*, and always to the left of the *Key* card.

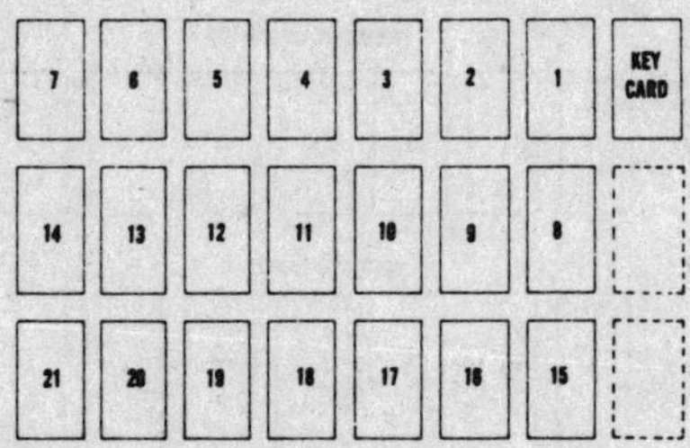

The Diviner reads the meaning of each card from *right* to *left*, both individual cards and groups of cards.

G—THE GYPSY CARD SPREAD

The Diviner separates the 22 Major Arcana cards from the 56 Lesser Arcana cards and gives to the Questioner the 56 Lesser Arcana cards. The Questioner shuffles the 56 Lesser Arcana cards and deals out in a pile face down the first 20 Lesser Arcana cards. These 20 Lesser Arcana cards are put together with the 22 Major Arcana cards to form a 42-card pack. The remaining 36 cards are set aside.

The Questioner shuffles the 42-card pack and deals out the cards in six piles of seven cards each, face down, beginning from right to left, so that the first seven cards form the first pile, the second seven cards form the second pile, and so on.

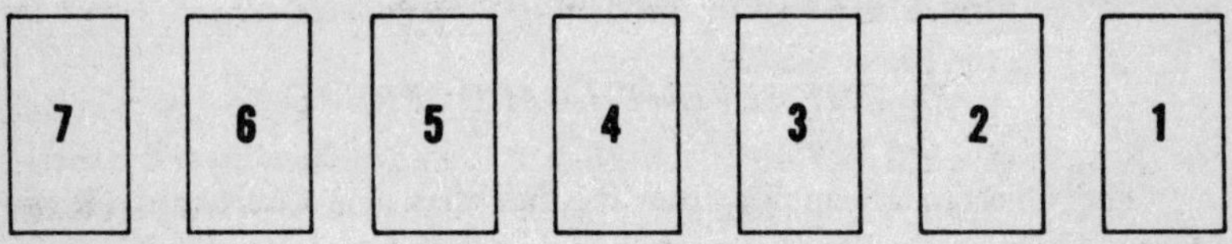

The Diviner takes up the first pile and deals out the seven cards, face up, beginning from right to left in a row of seven cards. Then the Diviner takes up the second pile and deals out the seven cards, face up, beginning from right to left, in a new row underneath the first row, and so on until there are six rows containing seven cards each.

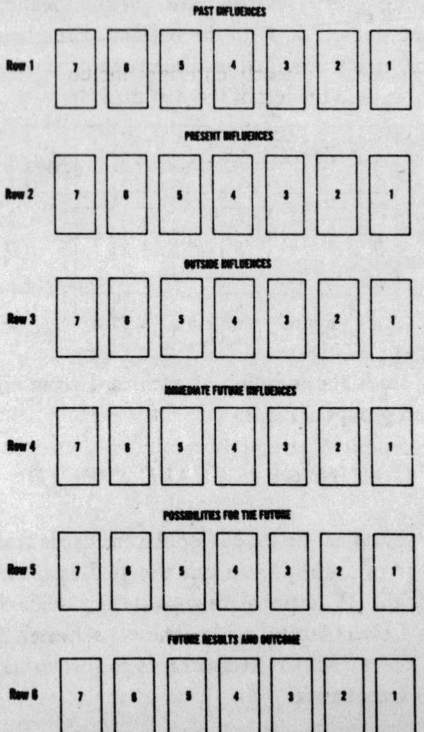

The Diviner reads the cards beginning with the first row by describing the course of events in general terms for each of the rows:

Row 1—PAST INFLUENCES. Those influences and experiences which occurred in the past and which have played a part in the life of the Questioner.

Row 2—PRESENT INFLUENCES. Those influences and experiences taking place at the present time in which the Questioner is currently involved.

Row 3—OUTSIDE INFLUENCES. Those influences, environmental factors, pressures and other outside events which are taking place and over which the Questioner has no control.

Row 4—IMMEDIATE FUTURE INFLUENCES. Those events and influences which are approaching the Questioner or into which he is presently entering, including unexpected events.

Row 5—POSSIBILITIES FOR THE FUTURE. Those events and influences which are available, attainable and avoidable by the Questioner if he wishes to prepare for them or avoid them.

Row 6—FUTURE RESULTS AND OUTCOME. Those events and circumstances which will ultimately result in the future of the Questioner.

The Diviner should bear in mind that the 22 Major Arcana cards in this reading represent stronger and more compelling forces than the Lesser Arcana cards.